Miniature

Miniature

Mac Wellman

ROOF BOOKS
NEW YORK

ISBN: 0-931824-03-7
Library of Congress Catalog Card No.: 2002100656

Back cover photograph by Timothy Keating.

Thanks to Yaddo.

Roof Books are distributed by
Small Press Distribution
1341 Seventh Avenue
Berkeley, CA. 94710-1403.
Phone orders: 800-869-7553
orders@spdbooks.com

 This book was made possible, in part, by a grant from the New York State Council on the Arts.

NYSCA

ROOF BOOKS
are published by
Segue Foundation
303 East 8th Street
New York, NY 10009
segue.org

CONTENTS

I: SCRATCHY

If it is was, parsleyworm, you happen
too
pinks'
ter.

WHITE CREPE-MYRTLE is to today
an X, throws heat
at a A
tapered dolly-winch
go up and, go
till the top

X greats and grows

a heart say.

Show?

Knee-
dull, cross

thorn, A

WHY the sand-pile physics resemble the
XY recorder my
rosy output device,
rows and rides
to
be
C: an 11 foot crocodile (*leidyosuchus formidabilis*)

granular objects
if jiggled resemble
a
mimic self.
Current zipzapzuptheory cannever
X
plane. Y.

—institutionshawalecturer1/4in theater
Zmore specifically 9 as HasRteacherz inthe
—ancient, Wdiscredited o/ low, fcraft
O This Iharddfate {came to nme.

FORD some___time now I HAVE LABOREDr at Q
Various of the 2b
etter Yclasspof.

IS it quite like a skingame, old devil,
in your Cromwell Chair
or lathing an axe
as an illustration
to an X;

is it quite so so? You
Mister John Podsnap
observing
the plupurplish skinkle

on X the Y, or on Crooke's Layer

a sphere of drink, a skink

of every ever Y. For

O is O forgone. And Y?

IS is it or say not and B's
a
pollen
toon. Weapon or tool

Cross to the, tired unbegun

Where
was
it that skink of mystic water

a skinkle on her topmist, drilled
by duskstar & Y.

CREPE-mist the inchmaster odd's
ball
to
a
cynic

Who gotten is guessed

at? Who
? If not

's air's

                    Too much and speaking masks the tell
                              till tooled

                            and retooled

                            X to X that

                           jagged zigzag

                       that golgotha'd Oresme.

DO THEY? Do the Tube-Alloys do the dark
jest
as an X was fiddled
into

searingcrackledsmoke

a Y away

A dark jest
within
who's
human chest?

                                        SPENT ONE, who or X
                                    what cry-stick or crysystem
                                    fuels the mules, spent one
                                                           hole
                                        life, Lear, spent one
                                       learning to fuel the,
                                         the charge the, X
                                        to love the wrong
                                               charge the

MILLS OF ARTAXERXES.

                                            To charge the
                                        Mills of Artaxerxes.
                                         O pisk, O pask.

                                                      The

                                   A wrong woman, wrong'd.

Inwit to bite's aglitter
with Gideon's low blow, o

the corporate X

corps'd its grow

with quite the lilliputian L.

Hell is

not, X, a hole below.

Airy, the moon's rock-stubble face absorbs all
my X my light zag's zim zum
&
dark the final
countenance
till
up tilts
a
poor thrush Y.

Y fiddle when the bluebeard'segg dozes
in
the,
the nest
of hollow wives
on moon-raked
hyacinth
coiled
behind the hearing
    socket.

            The high strung Poindexter Arch of no
                  self un
             begun and no to doing
                undusts a Sphinx

              track after slow track

           under the dusty riddle's

                   writ

        an O perfect by no measure, man.

Airy I've YEARNED my white right:

So, so

that room my bond

empty so quite

a day was, is.

No's night. Long

Tell me, said the X to the— Answersoap
what is was the Airy Thing
supposed to be supposing
in Crowe's Dark Space
an ent or an hinge

An hinge, replied the North-

stone, as it shall be;

no, as it were shall be;

Southerly— a simple medication
can get your call caw caw
through
Any O time.

Time to, till
Flawless, sit
thing or standing.

Those are these pants.

16

An episode of no to interrogate some
former blue
eye, Mister Crime of the Century
of you
dulcet
ever
lucid, ever X to Y
ever
acqua

shoes.

Boule d'Or
bowl
upon the wingwindow

hear less, then more

Airy spaces fill
the

23 kinds of mortgage fall down

X before the

II: ALL POSSIBLE HATS

X's radical reboots to a blues beat

listen how a greenslip

face offers to me a deep Y storystonelip.

The Great Wall of China pot
grecized
X's
the old girl network, deep
in deepest things, an

argent relic

wherein the whys of its actual condition

reluct a gree

                              Greasy spoon huddles in the X

                                        Great vowel shift,
                                                       gre.

                                                 So silver
                                                     goes.

So, as here up and there, soft
devil's
fur
is

no more, but flame of flitters
puffs.

So, in the word restless
one
duress is

X enacted by the hepcat's

philosophunculism.

Crowsfoot's philleroo is a jest in

airy X's duress

of no

goings on

a

way

Genitor's stomachache aes triplex
in
no X's nope:

Egg and dart
Egg
and dart.
Egg and
dart.

The mole's hip betrays carnal lever
assemblies

with a double-dutch

down
under
the
deep Plutonic

bim, bam, bum.

Reynold's Morbidezza screens what Bat
did and
Bat did not do,
Dull Care, X-ray to Dreamland,
Fly

to awful's wordtrap and shuffle

X's

Connecticut transfer shade the
soft
glazes for Jersey Shore

Face the
X
trouble trouble-tuned:

Willy-bugs was here first

Philargyry, that
philocubist,

does it
en-
candle

the Dome of mysterious
Hem-line?

Know it now.

Just as your crippled ounce

replies ad nauseam

ad infinitum uncovers

your true fool's gold; goldensocks' earful of

all possible hats.

The slouch is an incorporation of its
canned heat.

Covered rage boils in Tom's
door.

Matted fur fills the house by

you know where.

All possible hats

bound and X

piffle.

The CROWE who taunts Webster's bagpipe
taunts in vain.

                    Raven's Way
                        tilts
                     to a un
         finishable ragtime colloquy;

              I hear it all, sad

                 Bee person,

     and am lifting, like a wand, by some

             perfect higher wood

                    aglow

                    YOU who practice a certain Burton
                    rubber processing in your dreams
                    deserve a better set of springs.

No telling who. No telling what.

Who and what
stay that way
despite the telltale alteration.

Shut up with an unholy
truth.

X is; but so is Y.

Y cannot fix a stare that is a soonly
hyper mended X, for

the meaning of the rule Stands Apart.

Absolute gridlock rules the
empty intersection. No semeiotic

covers the man-orchid's
imbricate.

Fond Poseidon rehearses sleep
but it is
death who, yes,

hears and responds;

X upon X^2. It is

why the seas are mad;
possess no god.

Suddenly so, so tarnished
by an oddity's resemblance.
My dreams are
witless weeds.
They indwelling, scheming
in all the rare earths;

take over all parts of the sad
world's diversity niche.

NOTORIOUS Marine Discount supply
is not rigged
to
recognize you,
Blue Jones.

Pray elsewhere, with your cash
receipts.

III: ODD'S BOP

In this WORLD every single other
who wants out;

as if, poor Deuteronomy,
the way out were an

acrostic.

You cannot measure
and listen too;

nobody gets their poor leg
up and hurt

beyond
the fact nobody's
abridgement

tips us off, on.

                              Day with her scarlet beard
                              inaugurates a new world;

                                 an old word actually,

                                    retooled like the
                                           formula

                                  I chose my own
                                           name

                                      among: a

peekaboo system grafted on Pepper's ghost.

Airy

is a no know nothing tattler
on a lark.

She is to X, as

you are to the stable of your
in
dwelling apparatus: all

gas, working class gas.

In some dark place, a cornered
weasel
snarls, rips at
a puppet rat;
as off just

a bit the macquereau
has it
wrong: the
rat ripped at

called not Jesus, while he in the desert

returned a solar
grimace. These are days

Long ago, as he, too, ripped at something raw, something awful.

Instances not well served
by
Macleod's gauge.

Are you, Airy, an oblate
or prolate
spheroid?

Silliest speculation
arms the proleg

Time unhinges
what we do
with;

spun around a darning needle
in the dark
like

so much yarn.

Rider's X is
an
open vestibule before
the cello
phane.

Pronaos, protect us

from Airy's

flame.

Gladly, my eyes turn from a site of ruin
to happy nomenclature.

Too few ravens, this time, to square the

next year's dire cube.

Ticklish Airy
humors
the
gong on a gong show of the

mind; for the

lightgong going out is no

fickle feather.

37

A silvery wood, in the blush of night,
hath no second nature.

The dreaming relic
recomposes

nonself Safety Supplies.

Each lie joins the banquet
wreathed
in tall gold

like a slipper, standing on
her toe.

Bold light, coldest of the cold knowers
and deceivers,
stay the mimic
X
of your radiant Y;
leave me be
like the radiant Man-Orchid
I read about
& concocted, in vain,
to fix
what is what &
curiosity had been, had to be
broken.

Error's reproach is wonder's redoubt
as
if
an if
were
faintly
a why.

Forward we fly, unthinking
new from now, time
unbidden.

Lightly we dare to claim desire
not her effortlessness;
untried, unproven and perhaps untrue.

Banish myth-willow to the witching hole
as
a
case
to
be driven consequent and madly

teachable. Oh, empty,empty

pinhole of wordy
toots,

what's too teachable's untrue.

Whose shut eye, far away,
wakes me up
as if
these silly things were true.

And I were
not a

skip it, and wish for more,
Rider.

Neutral in a war of doubt and
truth I

test the minefield
with a toe

only inky night
could love

proceed blind unblinking.

                              Airy's delight canned
                                                  is
                                         air deprived
                                      of consequence,

                                    and consequence
                                     of even a mouse's

                                                 de-
                                               light.

        All odd names slumber in the same
                        nest, unloved
                              and
                            distant

                    from suburban tents
                      of the teachable,
                      of the doable:

                    Banal naturalism's
                          natural
                         internet.

People who think writing is the
heart unhidden
have forgotten not just where
they hid the damn
thing,
but why, for Pete's sake,
Y.

Of here, on full, to be
better there;

an answer that

unanswers doubt's

double nonself.

IV: HEYWOOD THE HUNGRY

My fixed wheel wobbles on, un
knowably

herself, an

item selvage crow to

dispossess of X. Oh, to

dismiss the tenses.

Leave, your Airy interlocutors, both
upper
and darkest rickety places
to the sooty-footed prowl of
Heywood the hungry.

Knowing not, dear X, what to do
the shoe of bitter knowledge
leads me forward into the realm
of binding arbitration.

Not a true X, but a feasibility study
in
doability
studies
has

an imperfect hexagram

peering down the hollow
cube

thorn rules with beet & juice.

Airy's single error was to attempt
to name the sparseness
between X and Y, domination sisters.

Big Head, Cathy X, Leilani
of the wooden hands

what is humanity

We meaning you

using a presence to create
gestures.

Beryllium and chase
your tail.

Forbid us thing, and that we
peekaboo,

on X for to Y and

why not?

                    The tamper "dare" is a hampered
                              elf

                    eleven stories off the

                         yground.

Note my hem, saith Lady Fall, as
if
we dumb people's
mind darted
like our
smoothy jazz.

Old shell game, remind me why
my
name is Airy's
if
where I go's a mysterious
excess of crisscrosses.

Give me Full Service Parts and I will
channel your
turbulence
two at a time
like broody oxen.

I prefer this end vacant to that
one full.

Vacant theater talk

An O.

Tumble, and be
greatly
unhinged: the

art to aspire to the vortex
paradox
streaming forth
from infinite horizontals.

I did not occur to me at the time
of our
last parting;

and so

no agreement has reached
the point of part,

not agreeing to
insist on lasting.

Time, like Airy's self-indictment
repairs all tears in her fabric
with
effortless, and almost unbelievable
brevity.
Time's old
trick is all
this is.

Silvery, a golden eye is my error's
sole surviving
shadow and
place devoted to the folly
of full concealment.

Cancelled accrual and a whip
of darted invoices;
the true telling receives a voice
despite what
all
that interest
amounts to.

Flight, which was escape, now is
a mere saw,
and dangerous wide-faring
high over heavy-bottomed yarth.

My notion of millennium
is mum
on omens.

Time's an ocean.

Fundamentalist shade has Raven's
number
guns the tom
cat

to exponential aubergine.

You ask, and what next
and
after that,
what is next and

all that matters is a
slide, side-ways, through
the apparent's
customary view-finder and so

one forgets what the
question was.

My silly art's greatest gift is to have
stopped the
devil's blowgun
with a cork.

Shallow, hieratic dish, on night duty,
why
spill your flame
on idiosyncratic
me, if not to
mock the Socratic;
if not
to buck a trust,
to bend a rule,
or raise from the dead
a
lost
friend, like a wish unsaid.

See, a simple
initial ruled
by heart
to start the
starry sequence
of go and part;

I am to myself,
my own upstart.

Had I my central principle
intact
I should have lost
the
virginal impact
of the original lack,
the heart's apartment.

No less than you has doubled
me,
and cast the bone
of social security,

the number I cannot recall
that is my political identity.

Some slickered charm holds up
Airy's most
intimate underclothes;

the frost lingers, seven-fingered
only on her
tippy toes,

and on the sole remaining
Jalisco golden rose.

Who invented non-shifty Wolfish glide

if not
pale-knuckled Moriarty?

Do the heart and feather balance?
or is it a question
not of spring
and scale

but of an apparent
level, infinite and horizontal?

Or, one might say
the
heart and its feather
select a separate
set of equilibria
each

as each semi-second
succeeds;

And, like our larval hope,
mutates.

As, at the eastern end of the ocean
you call "The Peaceful",

the speaking leaf is skyugled.

The drop, a sheer one, starts up
at this puntilla,

where feather & heart
meet

in an exact scintilla
of doubt,
Love's redoubt

all on
gravity-feed.

                    Though the mark must stem the
                              way

                    the wound is not stanched;

                      a door is not a grave
                      even if departure,
                    on each scarlet occasion,
                       must remind one

                    at some point on the road
                      one must reach that

                        awful terminus.

What the scales do not reveal
of heart and feather is,

well, a

thing anterior to utility.
A restlessness
we

are less than human
without.

After, after, always after.

The sea is like a field of grass,
grasses the color field
mice would like to be.

After, after, always
always after.

A local genealogy tosses out to
Rabbit Man

a version of the truth.

Tooth, tooth, tooth.

O my green hat, what a
sun
day sat. Even for a mendicant

riddle
cat.

RELUCTANCE

For now keep reluctance
a day
on each;

the big judge has abated

now's strange
keep; leave the

hunt to mighty Torwell
far away,

and let this
day slant
now,

as now's to come

COLERAINE

Go back to what, what heightens as

the families of Limavady

one tree, no eyes,

ruinance, as if

shadow crossed time.

    ~

    Not much left, in full abeyance

    till, till

    the hatted what comes

    comes clean to
    —

    Too, too

    to clean what's hatted, the

    henceforth.

    ~

I plant
the bomb but
the

exact place where,
well,
it walks off somewhere else
than I
intended.

     ~

Hop to hates to name its name,
to be
by hope redressed,

all of mist and hiding,

as hope doubled, driven
redescribed.

An ought would have it.

Silly to be a chance

     ~

Something that is exact
a cone-tip

perfect stillness, at the same
time, time's

twirl, one

substance, both

aglide and motion
less.

     ~

Quite quits as ought would have at it;
a
shoe
less
feet.

~

Does does too sometimes do not do
what it
ought
in the nasty

(nasty nasty nasty)

nomenclature of what it

shoed? Should, I meant

should, not

shoed.

~

Something that cats chew on we
should, perhaps

eschew, as if something,

something

hung there, in the moment

like a shoe we
did not choose.

Because it did not fit as well

the cats knew.

~

My angle on the optic X is Y inched,
squared and snaggled;
to be or
fitted, straight-waisted; for the
coat's
deep pocket. I am all a hold
deep pocketed

My angle my apple
core

~

As M inched, was I so dusted, not even
ink
dries the frame;

not even my sad fame

can outlive hope. A

slow wind dandles the Spanish moss,

there.

~

Corruption's thistle is blind to mood

I
guarantee
you.

Not from righteous anger do the
untrue fly
but
from mood, philosophy's eye.
            ~
Circle hobby is crossed
eyeful

heaven to Miller's
Toot

too travel, too

scary to;

            ~

And and we are we double
doubtful? Say to

M, whoa

is early waxed, because
of love and

certain total hexes.

            ~

Demos ethos hath
 popped her crown.

            ~
After money stops being
all that funny

retrace my steps

to, to, to

    ...

two, two, two

    ...

I meant too, too, too

    ....

The rage of too. And find
not
one person, really, there.

    ~

If the divine is truly just
one
step behind

Can we hear
hell from
here?   How can

we know what to line
the sky up with?

.

The sky up with
stuff

pronounces a self
too

mingly for mindfulness.

    ~

Bird crows at the solar flash
point;

what's new's

news, and never

knows

how not to—

never knows.

~

As some
rain gathers up all things spiked
and flattened;

so the double-hedge teaches the
maze how to

hedgehog, how.

—

The long, low, loutish hedgehog bears
no
evil brow

to brunt delight;

he keeps his hindsight
behind him.

~

A shrilling tearing cry of the
lost or wounded rabbit;
the rain walks high,

high in the
abstract;
walks by rabbit cry and humped dune,
tall all unthinking.

~

The first connect has

us, la la, let down;

so too the second and third,

la la, the earth the sky;

all is, la la,

pointless, summed and

unsquareably so;

all have us, la la,

let down, down, down;

as a weasel sucks

eggs, as a

weasel

sucks eggs as a weasel

suckseggs

~

Perhaps what bears upon the
mighty cushion
fellows

a curse like that of chilled
blush water;

perhaps, just perhaps
heigh ho heigh ho

nor dandle the ragweed

if you dare to darn
wisp from thorny

thorn.

~

A savage splatter, waxen tracks
across
the star-crazed page:

What relief? What hope?

What riven image
snow
glow, and

hitherto bound?

~

Red tail

a-gait in

of the tempo
put, pat; put, pat; put, pat;

what nose

un-

wrinkles at

what white

crime?

~

Red head what's untamed and a
live,
are you, tell me, timely too?

~

Is the splatter blue wine or
next to mine?
A soul's
worth of plenty
wasted,

tossed, in plink plunk

the oldy hat

of Groaner's felt,

abstraction.

~

One way Bellarena flightless
dog
studio brown study
versus
an egret's out

~

Spatter of mud flats on

the way to
Bellarena;

what blush inhabits
that. That

too loose

splash of land lock?

~

Some thing that exacts the soul
to penny wise;

some other that sharpens
the dull

and dulls the sharp; eye

food is not, bingo, bengo,

the ear's

balpeen hammer.

~

Double up to triple threat and

face off, face up

face

out,

nearly, nearly, nearly, all

the way to

queerest

Limavady

where people do the scary

(scary scary scary)

walking all the way

on the blind end of a

wooden stick—

walks the walls, as if, of Derry.

All the all the all the all ...

~

As the huge crows of Coleraine are

instant situations
troubling to repose,

so to my own non selves,

I am;

each one a further hedged bet;

but over the hedge and over

another,

glowing in radiant blush-bluish

pursuit, the girl in the

glazed sunset, looks back

wide eyed, open mouth an O.

~

Trouble to take, something else

on a dare,

hedgehog, you;

you of the narrow face,

remind me how I am not

like you. But take the trouble

each blue moon, anew

~

Day

down to
inches'
spite;
white
day
upon no
periphery, for
upon the next
one, one
is
quit, who is
quite. My
onus be
a bonus

BAZZONE

BAZZONE SUPERIORE

1.
Ruined heap (Castello)
rises
at Siesta, for one
person only

thumbnail of the far

village

unshadowed place

what far

what sleeping
olive

~

DIRVTA, 1590, has blessed
too
this dusty swirl,
as it stands

Dove sta ...

2.
Terra cotta saint (1590)
as
voices
wake
the yellow heat;

feed the sweet golden
pear

to the tawny buck

he chases off the

others

wants it all
himself.

3.
Floor to what heaven,
transverso,
into, or at
Umbria,

reversed.

Umbria. Imbrium.

Inamorata.

The yellow cat's

olive ghost rattling the
faded

theatre frames.

Oh, fenced in one,

horned and hornless, why

do we do what
we do?

UH-OH

To live is to act.

— Isaiah Berlin

. . . uh-oh the Overthrow (The Argumenta).
sundisc has, ah, over
played the, ah,
Oversoul; has a
V valve lain with a
drastic sidekick and
there you are;

~

CANTO 1

Cooked goose of instep
overthrow
thrown as throne as throne can be
throne as thrown as throne can be
thrown as thrown as thrown can be
and no slide-rule
Reunionist has hushed the
matter Silvery's
sleight of hand
has caused to be
sprocketed. Has caused

to stay the splay,
retuse and sinuate.
Crowded

opera hats, recusant unredeemables
pardon the tails
reluctant top timbers
have caused, likewise, to appear
apparent to no other
fractured deity, but of whom
it is spoken: No gravel
grows under her torch-lily
toque, till the till
is filled with other scarcity,
debris of azure heaven, popped
out into a wastrel
dig, all top dog topery. The
end
of Uh-Oh is: I should've
griped
heaven's wingnut by the Western
most flange, at the Wendish
Outreach Station, there, by eld
Cubicular Heights, where the
pork pie greets the cowboy with an
alien doff, placating rebuff
and porism which says to

each, hold and stay thy
point. The Illuminist gaff's
broken wind, wind of tines
and screwier owls than are
fork
brother to screech;
brother to awful inappropriateness,
denier of Jesus Olfactory Depression
our seldom seeable
cereal
DeepSeatedOne, weighing down the nays
and noes of categorical
upstart. Of figman and figwoman

our curious and silhouetted
Types, tongued and tasselled
earliest of deodorized Earliers,
all cinquefoil, gullies
shrivelled like the short-tailed shrew,
to uttermost moonwort, a
thing no other thing can hold
honorably, in hand.

~

CANTO 2

For Time's jalopy and hosted mice,
gone whopping loose-strife, or,

loose-strife whopping and lost a wheel
to whosoever
has diddled crackery;
whoso has done that
ensorcelled act of not so bright
retrospection is a snow-man
deft, too deft to hear Time's
low-note rumble. Too populist
and other-fascinated, far the fair,
to settle in with, in a relativity incline,
Janus-faced, safe in the mistake
no no-man, old Porphyry's own,
has jacked and swayed,
sinless and slightly Roman
as though lost like a wooden top
on the silver-tufted current of Japan.
Japan, our western bezant,
similar in form to the classical
patera, especially on the fiascoes
of archivolt, pictured girls and boys
of the Japanese nation that

lost the war, but won the peace;
thrown as throne as throne can be;
throne as thrown as throne can be;
thrown as thrown as thrown can be.

~

CANTO 3

I was a Prowl Car
and a journal box
both; I
do as I am directed
St Finitude has ruled;
this corks the bottle
my syntactical boat
floats, with flagrant quintara.
Santara, santara, santar.
An "if" of proximal stress
relaxes; all our glory,
pruning hooks, deathward set
to horrify the cloacal;
find prunes for the metaphor
workers, sipping an ichor of shimmer
glow, in our dank, low housing,
all housing without siding
because Mister Shiloh missed his
mark at Mount Psychochemical,
a place, like Amor, not on no
known chart, a place
aped by the unlovely
shill, chosen sod of Hobson.
So when you slide downtown

with the Law of Menippus in your Wendish
knapsack, stop for a quick cafe

at my cousin Leaden Joe's.
He has beheld all fishes
that illuminism wonders
at, deep breathy phosphor tube-crocus,
amusements of ribbon, Niger Congo, feathered angelus,
sunken nidhogg, stooped enigma fish;
and the fabled eel of New Nickerie
who nidges, frames pantropical
ecotops, all roundly aglisten, gruff
and soiled in a mystic attar
no seemly utterance has space
in her vocabulary for, for
Pansy is a girl's name, not a
quadratic of release. But
the cynic is a fool;
the fool is a gimmick the cynic
has supposed a tool, but
Moses had perfect pitch.
Pray, relay to the infinite, my relator
this local delusion, this dust
as lost Seti deposed in Crete.
So
fetch only the waxing moon
to amend wrongdoing and the Law

Nations makes wrynecked, wood.
Wood is mad wood in wildish
dogmatic, so Miss Wyoming dreams
sewing up her lira in waxenberry
frenela; the girl there, so aware
St Finitude has longeyed, long, too
long, her golden hair, object
correlate, pigalle, homestead,
loadstar, coin of praise, folly, lust.
So: Do not ask for flint glass
when you mean the fabled
object ball. The man of war

like the periodic cicada, is drenched
in fantan and lilywort reverie.
Problems are posted for him
to consider, dry as infolded
granulate mica. Precious dust
the polyphemus moth conveys
All the way from Proverb,
France, a place September
massacred in one aloof
Mind. A mindful murdered thing
seeking the so and so
of romantic question and repose.
Rosella, rosella, rosella. Pose

                    ~

So and so, the Rose-Water man, SS
(Sunday School) reject poses in
rude rebellion to Any's ethical T-square;
this happens, late, by the dimestore
nickelodeon, Cubicular Heights'
one moral Rosetta Stone. Idiots
assemble to watch, lurianic
outlaws accuse the times
without a cloth and goth
processional. What the tale
that origin has obliterated, scone
and scone, mad Rosicrucian
hack fest, might seem to was as is;
therefore's failed theorem.
We bear the majestic scourge
thought cranks up, all souls,
eventual mandrake, blossom of rosehip,
a driven crie, fatal
parenthetical. Particular physic. An
oh.

This too shall
pass. Oh,
we all make mistakes, only
some uh-oh, all the utter clarity

down driven, ah, the fatal
cellar steps, one way
staircase to hell's
blue flower suite, limitless, solemn
dreaded tomb of the fieldmouse, owl even;
you who
dip in a phantom's disregard
for truth, no lake in Avalon;
place of welded swords, X
with no rights and no privilege,
a marked man in hearts, have a power
less for that garden path
shrouded with abominable tree branches, the
ray of hope raised in Xyst;
Solomon's
Rose of Sharon— luminous,
dripping a cold attar of phosphor,
slightly damp— and dead to worlds;
than a will to right what's tipped
over, all the way.

~

Passionnel, reveals a bookish
crime against nature; crime
the rawest parable of might crows,

always indelible, always at noon
time. Because you, the fairly wronged,
lost youth, have overmanned the
occidental with merely human
messages, guesses at the dark

pull the accidental causes
poof and overpoof, obscuring all
with all other pulled teeth, factual
noise. Irony
ironizes ironicity, and other
occidental nuisances.
Accidents are always certain
they are to occur just when and whim
crimes against nature are true
in this absolute manner. The way
cleared for the human by a formal
contingency appalling as the idol's
smoke, santara santara—
Santap. Law reduces only the lip
tragedy adheres to; all the rest
engorges the human sky like an
unpredicted unexpected violence
storm, santara santara—
Santap. Of the sort no one here,
all dental throwbacks in star
or four-points' region, can recall.

The Law stands outside the law;
what is foretold does not demand
to be told when to fold up tents,
curse the wild raccoon, and get
Gitana in out of the rain before
she is absconded wholly in that wind
gin,
a thing gone,
unafraid girl
just the way fearful Elementals like
them. Slender waisted, pale— and to
wit and knowing wholly dead. Songs
like to dwell on these conclusions;
total removals, speech without a hope
of pindownable edifying star-scatter.

It is after all, La Mama Umbria,
a dark time we keep telling
ourselves we have mistakenly got
ourselves, lost in a pigsty, in.
— humiliation. Wolf moaning;
then a girl comes out from a tree.
She smiles, slank. Once more
everydayness has shanked reality
and she cannot get away.
Smiles, slanker. More good-humored
than he who set the top

to spin, maddened wooden isotope,
had he been, thus, sprung. She
cannot go; still, she is too fair
to stay. Fair meaning just.
In the woods we hear someone we thought
less than us, make a better music
with a stick, a bucket and a window pane.
Pika, pika, pigweed, pike. Pika Pika.

~

CANTO 4

Airy's wish is to complete her education
unafraid of willybugs. Wish for Oversoul's
underbelly and walkable tangents.
The cosmic geometer has slept through
our false damnation, she thought. Apparently
I am finished. It is this perhaps
the point St Finitude adduced, wakerife
midrib, involving the Wendish rule
no one had ever yet invoked, without
or within the saint's earlymost nest
on Lower Rupert Isle, a place of inky
black leather ribbon-fish, and site of certain prehistoric

rites, all night rites
of seven, eleven, and bright pink pumps.
I deduce a closing

door, thought Airy
her nose climbing like literary judgment;
Kicker's parabola is veering this way;
Very's hyperbola turns my song to hay
hoots of a primitive ball
game. Not baseball but backswimmer
balky. Ballarat, ballarat, ballarda.
The balance
bar has catched expressman's rifle.
Coldest summer in a hundred years
they say. How do they know? Who,
who, darn it, darn it, has crept
out of the baccarat to proclaim this
if not owl's Blagg, a crater in the first
quadrant of the moon, not known
for making tracks in outer dark upstate
nettled underwood. Blagg, two miles
across, a blast crater two miles across,
home to none but ghostly homeruns
of Honogiru (of Cipangu),
sixth son of Nono, bar sinister
boar's head erased, stag's head cabooshed.

~

CANTO 5

Silver knot, slink-square in the dire rope.

Rope of fiendish mold people, fssh.
Yes fssh and nddlg. This last an old
oath on the truancy of certain beans.
Cranberry beans driven to choose

where to go and whether to become, like us
a kind of people. People, less and more.
People, and thus subject to a rule
that cannot be adduced outside
the hat of that, Kerygma's Enigma,
star fruit of the eldest known elected
knot. Big one. O Spinnaker
of myriad Kepi, to what dark fulcrum
do we tend? do we doom toward?
So we do the Dinwiddie be-bop do-wop
with an erring sense of wardour.
Recalls me: Wardour's wobble
a kind of fanatic diorama we used to
(not Airy, not Silvery, not me certainly)
frequent in our
kicks and cartwheels, proclaiming
for all Love and Justice and other
similar causes, essential and dimorphic,
inked to a local disturbance plate;
blue lightwave at the bottom of the lake,
Lake Zannagustapolier,
where at midnight the mighty ratfish blow,

bellow and blow and blow once more;
fates are facts twisted to hard knots,
strangulation napkins, 7
kinds of forbidden veils, 3
kinds of inner light handkerchief,
the ones we give in trade to Feather'd Peoples,
whose dark, runcible nomenclature
is permeable to our, inly
ownest, Newtonian wishes. Those
we improve to help
the Fall. Those
Who were mostly like
us before the
Fall

fell, awfullest Transparency. Awful
clearing in the antique woods of Cubicular Heights.
A place like any other, roundish
and cloth-covered, a-thrill.
...
Statement of worth, crossed, crossed out,
Belcherized. Rendered snotly
by dwarfish intervention.
Cruel Ilka, your hand-springs have
lain these long years in wait for pretty
Susan's bum;
there is no rule to caution, the localism

is supreme, is's infolded after
works. The setting down within strange canoes,
overminded ministrations, cuckoo
taunts, night's cahoonery, all
crickets, doves and foxy
squabble, a parliament of squeaky hinges.
There is no right rule to any of this,
Airy, what opposing FICT
with undenominate FRACTION supposes. It is all
Luther's cool blown. Burbank's possessive
shawl exposed to the Arctic sun, bleached
and kept for clean by the
Northmen. Their guess's good as mind.
Cush, cush, cush, cush.
Inly owns a fractured inch
and not a kind of fiddle-faddle,
for night is mind.

~

CANTO 6

Goat's rue and Goa powder
stand alone, an offering to the Ilfrit;

the rest of us sheltered from the cold night
by a meteor shower Sitt al-Husn the
Innocent mentioned but once, blackly,
in her bloodred Book. The fully human

error is built upon the twisty staircase
that starts on the plain, starsent,
at Old Sarum; Wends again. An
inmost of elsewhere, all
troubled by rounds. Place to place
moving with a fixed plan, Dorobo,
Wandorobo, Walvis Bay— the
Ilfrit's Ilfritah, scorched to cinders
by charged volts of Allah's
quiver. She who took our care much
to heart. Lost above the wandering Ghats.
No one's gain, no one's wamefou.

~

CANTO 7

On the wane
is waning, quote the cryptic Ilfritah;
want's wanion
is quite due to produce new
urges. Urges beyond the alligator
press, curse of the four-eyed devil
deep. Urges composed of simple
wishes. The common want of simple
things, things that bring a certain
piety to human dwelling. Places
not on the hit wire agenda.

Ghost places, old Zebu fear has accidentally
burnt out
in, leaving them alone and pretty.

Buttercups, phlox, foxglove and wallcreeper's
delight, all
spaces given over to children's
laughter, nameless beast chittering
that missed the epic upheaval
just next door, Site B, where fires smoke out
in ruined barns, skulls. Airy's
loss is Silvery's baccarat;
the offcast recast as the Savior
of Wands. Hairs'
jubilee. Idiot's true listening box
and bacca macca of citronella,
a surd of substantive
beyond the and of Babu Eliot's ken,
Signor Sterlino's. The hook-edge
of Nictu
viewed optimistically as Dawn's
Razor and day's bachelor degree.
In the woods at the city edge
no one takes the time
it takes to talk about these things;
old useless errors fill up the air
ways with the songs of hatred,

Tom Thumbery of Vengeance Deified
and the litany of dread. I sit
here. My car won't start and, hey,
it is not even my own car. Clearly
is someone else's and how did
I get into this?
And, hey, if
Police should come along and want to
know whose car
Would I be able to tell them?
No. No. No. God keep you, small and nicked
says the good
phantom Ilfritah. Angel of the soul's

removal, scotched egg of doom.
Unlike Socrates to Crito, I spew,
Then say: *Apeleuthomai euthus!*
which means something like
"Henceforth I'm out of here". And go—
after tossing high the keys over the
squushy green center of Lake Cristina,
shadow place. Yawn of unfinished
tasks, epic and otherwise. You? You guess
what Ilfrit saves me from my actions.
A thousand and one thoughts
occur to someone much wiser than me.
I correct myself, vault into the midst

of air and light and destiny.
Cuckoo cuckoo cuckoo gala cuckoo.
A mighty raintree ratfish rises and
with a blow of steam
swallows the keys, high, at the top of his arc,
splashes into the greenish moss
colored splurk, all the curled water
faints and refrains and refrains, still.
Other owly eyes greenopen doors and
shut eyes, other eyes than those
known to the othereyed, the green bottle,
bag, ball, belt, bay, barked acacia.
Briar, crab or dragon. Green
verditer, my greenish strength.
And off some wolves moan
as the water stills,
comes to thick closure. And the, ah,
Elementals prepare for belief of the
predicated unbelievers. Those who are the
clueless. The many of church going
stopped ears, with mouths agape
in a stoppage of utter
wonderlessness, when! O Stars Above!

— humiliation. More wolf moaning;
then a girl comes out from a tree.
She smiles, slank.

Starts start
and
we rest on what's rickety.
Fssh and nddlg. After the "rickety"
an information burst of the untimely
as it burst upon you. One
soul among many, forever lost
to the FACT
We are all cuckoos in another's nest.
For night is mind
and not a kind of fiddle-faddle.
Inly own's a fractured inch.
Cush, cush, cush, cush.

ANTIGONE

PERSONS OF THE PLAY a n t i g o n e:

All parts are played by the THREE FATES, also THREE FACTS, on their way to becoming the THREE GRACES; with the exception of ! ∃, THE SHRIEK OPERATOR, (pronounced "E shriek") an unknown god of unknown origin; who is named for the special symbol of logical notation as described in the appendix of The Cambridge Dictionary of Philosophy, 1999 edition. The traditional parts are: CREON, ISMENE (ANTIGONE's sister), CREON'S son, HAEMON (ANTIGONE's betrothed), CREON's wife EURYDICE (in my version also the prophet, TEIRESIAS), and a CHORUS of Theban citizens.

———

. . . and on the roof of my head ...

:Mazzy Star

ANTIGONE

PART I [red bullet]
Once, at the beginning of time, the three Fates, unpleasant young
girls, enacted the story that was to become that of Antigone. The
three girls played all the parts with hats instead of masks, and a
whole rack of customary costumery.

A battle field. Heaps of dead clothing. Dead clothing strewn all
over. Three girls watch from a distance. Unknown god as a bodi-
less shadow approaches. As a swirl of fabric. I am the Shriek
Operator. ! Ǝ. I am the unique situation. I am the uncanny and
have come to this place, place crowded with corpses and the
stench of death. I am the Shriek Operator and am very pleased
with all this slaughter, this horror, this misfortune. Misfortune out
of contrast, sprung hinges, what creaks, what is fundamentally bro-
ken. Sand pours without anyone willing it. Pours from above.
From the sky. Something is covered. Something mangled and
horribly dead. Pours. Horripilation. Who. Who did this? I am
and I am not named Antigone, daughter of a man whose name.
The one of whom it is said, he possessed one eye too many. Saw
too much. learned too little from what he saw. Incurious.
Curious, how incurious. Mind made up. Driven from place to
place by ! Ǝ. The Shriek Operator. The shorthand for "... there
exists a unique situation ...". The shorthand that stands in total
contradistinction to the shorthand for "it will always be that".
Shorthand for "it always was that".

A song: Thus, it always was/ thus it will always be that/ thus, if I
am named/ who I think I am/ I will always be caught in the terri-
ble terrible/ cat's cradle. For I// both must and must not/ bury
my dead brother,/ Polyneices.

A Chorus: Of all things strange, humankind/ is the most
strange./ The cat's cradle/ is news to the spider,/ for all things go
round and round; for/ I was a stranger and you took me in; for/
I was a stranger and you took me not in; for// straw, straw, straw,/

99

straw shows which way the wind blows,/ and an empty belly thinks the moon is green cheese; for// (the King of Spiders)// Up he was stuck/up he was stuck/up he was stuck/ and in the very upness/ of his stuckitude/ he fell.// (Straw, straw, straw, straw.)// And what I learned from my long/ life of spinning string,/life of measuring string,/ life of snip, snip, snip:// You can't beat something with nothing.

Creon watches her. I wonder what she is. Doing in her thinking. He says: The rule is: Eteocles, hero. Polyneices, the logical opposite: traitor. If one, then not the other. This is an unanalysable truth. Truth is true. (That is why it is called the truth.) A rupture. Time backs up and shakes itself like a wet dog.

I am a stranger, Ismene, my eyes see the clearest. I'm clearing out. As she goes: Devil take the hindmost. Antigone. A hint's as good as a kick. Take the double-faced mask (that they were wearing). I see so clear I don't need one. What I need is a good hat. A fatal hat. She puts one on. She carefully balances an egg on one end.

3 Fates dance the Dance of Hollow Time and Hollow Earth. Everything hollow with a hole in it. Earth and sky. Ocean and the. Vast, electromagnetic carpets of stars and eggs and all possible hats. Celestial eggs. Egg egg egg. Most eggs are electrical in some way. Most aren't. Let's turn her in. Who? Antigone. Let's turn her inside out. See what god. You can't carry an egg in two baskets. You can't be in the same place at the same time. You simply can't.

She did it. Creon, she. Did what? You know. The bad thing, at the bad place. She buried him, or tried to.

A Chorus. Let us invoke/ the rupture of silence in the hollow of uncanniness.// Let us invoke/ the pause before the rupture of the already known in/ the presence of the already dead.// (Gods love to collect at the place of the dead as though it were a compass focus)// Let us invoke/ the arrival of the gods and the dissolution of all/ that is merely human.// Let us invoke the pause before the silence before all of this;/ for earth, hollow earth,// (hollow, hollow, hollow)// is the house of the dead, and the place/ of engendering. The branching of facts,/ facts which are opposed, contra-dictory./ Dog and cat facts.// Let us invoke/ the howl before the primordial howl. Let us invoke/ the spider that taught the spider, the/ very first one,// How to be a spider./ How to creep./ (And be creepy). They all do the spider. They all howl. They all creep.

A Chorus. Humankind is the most terrible,/ the most terri-ble of all things./ For/ when you step on your own head/ it is time to go home, and harmony/ seldom makes a headline./ Some wheelbarrows are red, but/ all insects have antennae/ for the name of an actual world is pronounced 'a round'/ once you allow the Facts to slide// (Slide, slide, slide.)// All down the slope to chaos will glide/ and what is not yet hidden/ will learn to hide, hide, hide/ and to abide// (Hide, hide, hide)// There on that slippery slope/ of the terrible unbidden, oh/ that I had in the wilderness of logic/ a place for wayfaringmen/ Those// Who mind the difference between/ things that are, and things that are not/ things that are, and things that are not/ things that are, and things that are not.// Hold on Antigone, hold on./ Abide, you bride of silence. abide.// Coda:/ Save soap and waste paper./ Two pizzas for one low price.

Creon as Antigone arrests Antigone who is Creon. A confusion arises. Someone does something. All change hats. Nothing feels right.

———

This includes what is buried. Harvest, ingathered by lightning, in view of all. This was done by Antigone, her, a bride of quietness, one of the *symparanekromenoi,* one of the living dead.

Verdict. Interment in the house of death, while yet alive. Agon. Antigone. In her geode.

Chorus of ordinary citizens. Well.... Eleven don't make a dozen. Give 'em an ell and they'll take a mile. The end of the thief is the gallows. The end crowns the work. The heavy end of the match is the light end. Ask the spider. She knows. They fall silent and dance the Dance of Charm and Distance. Silence. Pause. Distance. They dance the Dance no one has ever. They dance the Dance of Withdrawal. They dance a nothing dance. ! Ǝ The Shriek Operator appears. The hidden takes them all, perhaps. (... there exists a unique situation ...) Teiresias (played by Eurydice) appears. He is a man and sometimes not. Creon

Your offerings have been rejected. Creon: I do not have much information on this except the general statement of the Agency that there is nothing in the files to disprove her (Antigone's) communist connections [This is not a comment on communism; it is an instance of logical error.]. Okay. Okay. Eteocles, hero. Polyneices, traitor. That's simple enough. The news is what has been forgotten. The mystery. The absolute. The uncanny. The unanalysable, Creon. The unanalysable. Big words no one understands, or pretends not to. A little hole will sink a ship. A big old ship. A hole is nothing at all, but you can break your neck in it. No one can dig up a hole. Wisdom doesn't always speak Greek. The unseen, too. The incomprehensible. A wise man sees twice as much as he talks about. If things were to be done twice, all would be wise. Just let things rock along.
Haemon watches Antigone as she watches Creon. Fell in love with her violet eye. She thinks. Do the thing and have done with it.

102

Teiresias turns on Creon. Creon turns on Haemon. Haemon turns on Antigone. Pause. Silence. Pause. Antigone turns on Creon, as the whirlwind watches from out of the cat's-cradle. She says. Someone is always watching someone else, Creon. Someone is always overhearing. Why must this be. Each thing has a right place if you know how to place it. My brother's body, for instance. There is such a thing as motion in one place. Spirit is action. This attempted burial is re-action. You dramatize the issue. To dramatize is to think against the self. To hell with self, any self, yours or mine or another. I got my idea like you got yours. By watching another. I? A watcher? Precisely. You watched me and despise me for my clean, unpleasant spirit. I watched the burial of my brother by an unknown god. Death and crumpled paper. The true folly is the folly of burying the dead. May I go now. She goes. Fool. Fool. Teiresias goes: Those who speak truth, speak shadows. He that is not with me is against me. For every action there is a reaction. Disaster being the final logic of human action (Haemon). I don't give a damn for any damn man that don't give a damn for me.

A battle field. Heaps of empty clothing. Dead clothing strewn all over. Two girls watch from a distance. Unknown god as a bodiless shadow approaches as a swirl of fabric. I am the Shriek Operator. ! Ǝ. I am the unique situation. I am the uncanny, and have slunk to this place crowded with corpses and the scent of death. I am the Shriek Operator and am very pleased by all this misfortunate contrast, this contradiction, this contraction, because I am what lies outside language and therefore cannot be understood. Cannot be understood, do you understand? You are all housed in your unhousedness. The sand that buried Polyneices poured without anyone pouring it (... there is the unique ...). The unique is what is outside language and they dance the Dance of What is Outside Language. This is a dance of nothing. All go. The earth is dark. The nothing that happens now is the force that fills what is empty. All go except for Teiresias. Who mourns in a little Dance of Error and Disclosure. He says: Polyneices lived his death above the ground. Antigone below. The hidden take us far, far from the place we know, perhaps. A chorus: He who speaks of nothing does not know/ what he is doing.// In speaking of nothing he makes it into/ a something.// In speaking he speaks against/ what he intended./ He contradicts himself.

Another chorus: What is more weird than man?/ What is more weird than man/ and woman?// All mastery depends on motion./ Climbing the purple hills./ Driving through the mountainous/ seas. For even the purple murex/ lacks the red; for/ the bugle-cry of what's red is the/ pot calling the kettle black.// (Kettle, kettle, kettle.)// The hole and the patch should/ be commensurate, as the/ dog to his man should/ be obedient. It is as if I/ ask you to prove this bicycle/ belongs to Hector, and you reply/ "all the bicycles around here/ belong to Hector"; or the// fallacy of too many questions, the/ fallacy of affirming the consequent, or the/ fallacy of denying the antecedent, or the/ fallacy of hasty generalization, or the/ fallacy of irrelevant conclusion, or the/ fallacy of misplaced concreteness, or the/ fallacy of many questions, or the/ fallacy of accident; or the fallacy of bad faith.// What is more weird what is more weird/ than red feather than black kettle/ what is more weird.

Eurydice (played by Teiresias) walks in a slow circle. She is thinking of what to say to Creon. A part of the city has been swallowed by mud (we hope it's mud). A lahar it is called. Is this a god's dog's doing or what? Shall the hole in the center of the world be stopped by a girl? And not by the corpse of my son who fell in love with her violet eyes. Violent eye. We already know what will happen. Why? Why must we go into the whole damn piece of crapshoot playacting if we know the dice are loaded. Time does not like this remark. Becomes a weasel, or a vicious hedgehog, backs up, puffed up in raging horripilation. Antigone is stamping her foot. Teiresias as Teiresias: What are you trying to do? The three FACTS go in and out of a line like a. Like a cat's-cradle. The three Fates Alecto Megara Tisiphon. I am trying to stop something by stamping my foot. Omens are over. The signlessness of the omens is the most uncanny. Terrible, terrible, terrible. I am unable to stop thinking. Thinking of how to make a curse capable of ripping through human flesh like a goldarn bullwhip. We are surrounded by omens we cannot read. Surrounded by death and crumpled paper. News print we cannot read. All the print that fits the new, us, the walking dead, dead shadows. *Symparanekromenoi.*

Antigone. A witness to her own death. Thereby twice dead. A voyeur. A stranger in the house of being. Antigone: I am going to shave my belly. I am going deep into a hole. I am going to watch them. The ones who think they can watch over me. Deep in a hole and come out the other side. Place where things stand as they are. One two three. They follow her. The three FACTS, each wrapped up in her own fabric. Each carries her own dumb, expensive wand. Day. Night. Death and crumpled paper. Creon and Haemon are unable to speak to each other. Circle and stare. Watchers watched. Night says no to day. Silence.

Pause. A small unpleasant animal crosses the vast emptiness of infinite spaces. They watch this. Not a very nice animal, in fact.

Silence.

We behold, for the first time the curvature of the earth. Someone looks out and holds an egg. If X, then Y. Logic, someone says. A song: Thus it will always be/ thus it will always be/ thus it will always be;/ kettle, kettle, kettle,/ boil up a fragrant tea for me./ On the day of my final day/ on the anniversary of me./ The fatal anniversary of me.// Looks around, shivering and afraid. Look at her (this is a command). Alone and cold. No one to love her. No one to protect her. Nothing but stillness. Stillness laying waste. The laying waste of stillness. Now she is the focal point of stillness. And

and

and

and the gods are coming. Unknown ones and the unseen.

Collision of the necessary and insoluble in her girl's face. Each FACT denies another. All change hats. Nothing works. Nothing works, and the Rock emerges from the gloom. Castle Rock. In the middle of air. High above us. What is closed begins to open. Something catches us by surprise. It is Haemon, falling upon his sword, as is the tragic fashion. We hear his death agony. Slow way to die. Time passes unconcerned. His death is horrible. We watch him from a distance (this is a command). We feel nothing for him. We feel nothing human. We feel cold and alone. Antigone looks at us. We look at Antigone. Nothing moves us. Nothing moves

105

Antigone. This is the cat's-cradle. We feel nothing because we are no longer what's called "human".

A song: The devil wipes his tail with Creon's pride./ Listen to Little Jack fry up an eyeball for an egg./ Bubba tubba bubba tubba bubba tubba bup.// I am the kind of girl tired of always being wise./ I am the tin can tied to my own damn tail.// Fry up an eyeball for an egg/ Leg up, leg down, leg up, leg down/ Egg, egg, egg, egg, stupid old egg// Oedipus, he had one eye too many perhaps//Quietly, one of the three: I am the tin can tied to my own damn tail. Slow fade to black in which we hear them sing the song over again till they get it right. More right. Over and over. Silence

Pause. In which Time becomes a one-legged crow. Crow on a withered bough. Crow having a hard time cleaning her wing. Silence.

——

Once senses the presence of an unknown god. Then another. Then another. We behold for the first time (once more) the curvature of the earth. Once more the Rock appears. Castle Rock. In the middle of air. High above us. The Rock opens. A brilliant geode, violet and luminous. Antigone is enshrined within. She looks almost like a goddess. Which one? No man can say. No man can say. No man can say. How many can stay. And I slipped out the back and I made myself very small and I slipped out the back way and when I awoke. I was in a different place, a thin place, as though it were the place of a compass focus. And the lines of force radiated out from my heart in all directions and I could feel these lines of force as though I were a god and not merely a nasty girl, a girl tired of being the wise one. Radiated out from my still beating heart

•

And I travelled to the center of the world and and I made wicked-awful charms and devised ghastly rituals and some of these are for the propitiation of unknown gods. Unseen gods. Gods both unknowable and unseeable. For what lies buried in the center of the world are the last words of the barely alive but just about to be dead: Lord help my poor soul./ Jesu./ Give it (a candle) to me; it is time now./ Peace, peace, peace./ ...Addio, Mamma mia, addio, Mamma mia./ Edith./ It is very beautiful , but I want to go farther away./ I am not worthy./ Fire./ Moderately. I am continuing to orbit./ Death today, 66./ It is time.... Ay, Jesus./ Let not poor Nelly starve./ I want to go there./ Always. Always water for me./ Thank you, doctor./ Doro, I can't get my breath./ Well, if it must be so./ I am better now./ Don't give up the ship. Blow her up./ I have a terrible headache./ May God never abandon me./ Get my "swan" costume ready."/ I shall be glad to find a hole to creep out of the world at.

All now. And what lies buried below shall engender a time to come with many wonderful things. Let there be Spiders and Eggs and, and Hats, and gods. For all good things come in threes. Three Fates. Three Graces. Three blind mice.... Three dead Greeks. Dead Eurydice. Dead Haemon. Dead Antigone. And as I wondered, freely and threely, I thought I could see back to the old days at Thebes. She watches from within her geode. A place she calls "The Rat Minaret". Watches Creon and the Shriek Operator (! Ǝ). The one torments the other. City half buried in a tide of shit, Creon. Hey, Creon, look at me. Look at me. Creon, if it looks like shit, smells like shit, tastes like shit.... Hey, Creon, baby. Look at me. Hey, I got no teeth. I'm on drugs. He plays the washboard and sings a song: I've been a sinner, I've been a scamp,/ but now I'm willin' to trim my lamp,/ So blow, Gabriel, blow! Oh yes, Creon, yes, yes, yes. Of course we'll go back to Albania one day. But meanwhile we have to make a new life for ourselves at The Ritz. Whoopee! Creon flees. ! Ǝ The Shriek Operator flies after gesticulating with a meat hook.

———

Once, at the beginning of time, the Three Fates, young girls then, enacted the story that was to become that of Antigone. The three girls played all the parts, with hats instead of masks (well, maybe one mask is allowed), and a whole rack of customary costumery.

In this way they learned their nature and the nature of things and became the three Graces. Aglaia. Thalia. Euphrosyne. The one who gives. The one who receives. The one who returns. Three FACTS who are the three Fates who are the three Graces who are the three FACTS. Who are the three. Who are the. Who are. Who. The Fates turn into Graces just at the precise moment, Antigone, in their enactment, turns into a flame.

After the transformation they discover a puppet SOPHOCLES in a wooden box. Using an ear trumpet they recite the first stanza from the Second Stasimon, in Greek, into the puppet's ear (Actually, there is no puppet, only a girl's hand enacting the puppet).

There is wonder in his eyes; but there is much they will not reveal, much that must be withheld:

> There is much that is strange, but nothing that surpasses man in strangeness . . .

—

Lights up. They do something with expensive, stupid wands. Strange uncanny looks and smiles. First: To be positive: To be mistaken at the top of one's voice. Second: Fish and visitors smell in three days. Third: The play is finished.

Indeed it is.

End of play.

Almost.

Repeat the whole X 3 so that each may play ANTIGONE, each

CREON. So that each may be a whirlwind. Repeat X 3 exactly the same (only different). The first repetition, being partially erased, is seven minutes long; the second, only three. Silence. Pause. Silence. Now the play is truly finished (some may not think so).